LESSONS FROM THE CLOTH

501 ONE MINUTE MOTIVATORS FOR LEADERS

BO PROSSER and CHARLES QUALLS

Lessons from the Cloth
501 One-Minute Motivators for Leaders

Bo Prosser
Charles Qualls

SMYTH&HELWYS
PUBLISHING, INCORPORATED MACON, GEORGIA

ISBN 1-57312-252-1

Lessons from the Cloth
501 One-Minute Motivators for Leaders

Bo Prosser, Charles Qualls

Copyright © 1999

Smyth & Helwys Publishing, Inc.
6316 Peake Road
Macon, Georgia 31210-3960
1-800-747-3016

Library of Congress Cataloguing-in-Publication Data

Prosser, Bo.
    Lessons from the cloth: 501 one-minute motivators
    for leaders/Bo Prosser, Charles Qualls.
    p. cm.
    ISBN 1-57312-252-1 (pbk.)
    1. Leadership.
    2. Leadership—Religious aspects—Christianity.
    I. Qualls, Charles. II. Title.
    BF637.L4P66 1999
    262'1—dc21   98-30883
                                                       CIP

Dedicated to

Gail, Jamie, and Katie
for teaching me intentionality

Malcolm Knowles, Jack Naish, Mancil Ezell,
Chuck Bugg, and Harold Ivan Smith
for giving me vision

The congregations I have served
for helping me develop and emerge

—BRP

Elizabeth, the perfect partner in life and ministry,
for giving me perspective in all that we do

Mom, Dad, Jim, Janna, Ellen, Betsy, and the Boyntons
You are my family and roots.

—CLQ

Preface

Leaders are *not* born! Leaders develop through struggles and personal growth. Leaders develop as they come to terms with who they are and who they want to be. Leaders *emerge*!

The thoughts that follow are written to help "emerging" leaders. We don't mean to imply that we are experts or have life figured out. After all, experts simply know more and more about less and less! These thoughts simply act as snapshots of where we have been at particular moments as career ministers. We are emerging leaders, too!

Many of these words have come from our mentors. Some have come from life experiences. But most have been learned the hard way—through our own failures and from the failures of others. And, these lessons are still being learned. These words have personal meaning to us and have helped us in our leadership development.

We feel very deeply that lessons from church life should actually translate to broader fields, which is the way it should be. Business and industry have discovered that healthy organizations are built on healthy relationships. This is a sound plan for life. While the consistent, considerate approach to human relationships may sound old-fashioned or inefficient, this path does produce quality results. Healthy relationships rarely just happen. They take work and effort, but the journey is worth the investment.

These thoughts and philosophies may seem to contradict each other at times. They may sound backward. Our attempt is not to be overly spiritual or hyperbiblical. In fact, some will be disappointed that this work is not more like a Bible study—we'll let someone else tackle that. We don't intend to preach. We prefer to motivate positive relationships between the reader and co-workers, family members, and others.

Regardless of how many of these thoughts may follow, countless thousands can be added. We've even left some pages blank so you can add some of your own ideas to our collection. Enjoy these words of wisdom. Search for others. Share them. Live with them and by them. You will become more motivated. Your life will change. The choice is yours! *Emerge!*

Lessons from the Cloth
501 One-Minute Motivators
for Leaders

#1   Never sacrifice the happiness of the future on the altar of the immediate.

#2   Find 1,000 ways to affirm, praise, and appreciate people.

#3   If you stir up a hornet's nest for yourself, chances are you've stirred one up for your supervisor, too. Try not to cause messes for your supervisor.

#4   Invite others to help you remember and practice the concept of "partnership." In doing so, you are already partnering.

#5   Make peace with who you are. Make peace with your past.

#6   Dedication can rarely be measured with a tape measure.

#7   'Tis a wise person who knows he/she isn't.

#8 As the new person, find out what the hot-button issues are. They will be the launching pads for early successes, if you don't overreact. Listen to, learn from, and love the existing organization, and you will become the leader. These are keys to continued successes.

#9 Try *not* to forget where you came from.

#10 The person who seems to dislike you most may one day turn out to be your strongest ally. Then again, she may just dislike you.

#11 Always make friends with the bully if you can. If you can't, just avoid the bully.

#12 Never sell out just to make friends with the bully.

#13 Often the bully is just a person, beat up in another walk of life, who perceives some control in the organization.

#14 Often the bully is someone looking for a relationship but who doesn't know how to be a friend.

#15 Often a bully has found a niche of control and expects you to bow in homage.

#16 Hire for attitude; train for skill. If someone has a good attitude, you can always train them to do good work.

#17 If people trust you in public, they will reveal to you in private. If people trust you and reveal to you in private, they will praise you in public. If people don't trust you, they'll neither reveal nor praise you.

#18 If you are not the supervisor, notice where the person in that position draws boundaries between collegiality and supervision. You'll need to give him/her the space to be both to you.

#19 Don't mistake interest from your supervisor as permission for closeness.

#20 Never run from your problems; the names and faces may change, but the problems just follow you to the next place.

#21 Don't steal the organization's paper clips or pens.

#22 Mail your personal correspondence with real stamps. Don't use the postage meter for a letter to mom.

#23 Always say "thank you" in a personal way through handwritten notes and personal calls.

#24 A 5-line, handwritten note beats a typed letter on most days.

#25 When someone in need pops into your mind, let them know it with a note or a call. Usually, they need to hear from you right about that time.

#26   Trust your sensitivity and your gut.

#27   People go where they know, have been prepared for, and are cared for.

#28   If you are not the supervisor, don't let your care of the organization become a threat to the person in that position. Most will value your partnership.

#29   If you are not the supervisor, support the person in that position unconditionally. Let him/her set the pace. You follow loyally in service.

#30   Don't be a manipulator; be a motivator.

#31   There are two kinds of people in life: givers and takers. Be a giver, not a taker. Takers get more than they wanted in the end, including the ire of people around them.

#32 Someone thinks you come on too strongly. Someone thinks you are too meek. Someone thinks you are God's gift to the organization. Someone will be glad when you are gone.

#33 Never let a member of the organization draw you into talking negatively about a colleague. Be a partner in leading that person to have a constructive conversation with the colleague in question.

#34 Those who come to you speaking for "others" rarely are. Those who come to you speaking for "others" could be. Pay attention and choose wisely.

#35 Those who come to you complaining about "others" will also go to "them" complaining about you.

#36 If your friend gripes to you about his boss, someone in your organization is probably having the same conversation about you.

#37 Don't be paranoid (too much). Don't believe your "press releases."

#38 Don't neglect your family for the organization. Don't neglect the organization for your family. Balance, the key in most of life, will serve you well.

#39 Dress appropriately for all work situations.

#40 Time spent with the older members of the organization is well worth it. They are great sources of history, and your genuine relationship with them may help to move them toward tough change down the road.

#41 Listen more than you talk.

#42 When in doubt, ask questions. When questioning, don't appear to be in doubt.

#43 Model good leadership; lead the way you'd like to be led.

#44 Choose your battles. You can't fight them all, and you'll win even less.

#45 Posture all conflict so that everyone wins something. Win-lose situations mean that everyone loses something.

#46 Win little victories.

#47 Make 100 things 1% better.

#48 Choose extra carefully those things you would be willing to hang your job on. You will eventually get the chance to hang or be hung.

#49 Never fire a member of the organization if there is another way out. A move of that person to another place of responsibility and vision can solve a lot of ills.

#50 You probably can't be all things for all people.

#51 Unanimous votes rarely are. Secret ballots rarely are.

#52 Everybody is rarely against everything.

#53 Follow your heart.

#54 "Expect" your employees toward good behavior. It's better to err on the side of optimism.

#55 Step toward conflict early but wisely. Very few things just go away.

#56 If there is a pebble in your shoe, take time to shake it out before moving on.

#57 Be real with people. Laugh with them. Cry with them.

#58 If you venture into social friendships within the organization, know your boundaries.

#59 Never compromise someone with information they don't need to be responsible for. You can't take it back.

#60 Those who shoot for nothing usually hit their target.

#61 Don't overreact, overanalyze, or overplan. And *never* overstate.

#62 Never spend all of the organization's budget. Rarely will it all be there for you to spend. The budget is not a checking account.

#63 Add up the total of your vacation, sick leave, personal time off, and convention/conference time. Then try to develop a feel for how much of it you can allow yourself to actually use. Never use all of your leave time. If you do, you're gone too much.

#64 There is grace in the system. To the greatest extent you can, trust the system.

#65 If you have the chance to read somebody's memo marked "Confidential"—don't.

#66 If "it" couldn't operate without you, then you have probably failed in operating it.

#67 Run no farther ahead of your people than their vision and stamina can allow them to work. Bringing them along slowly beats working without them.

#68 Your urgent memo will rarely be read widely by your people. All errors, however, will usually be widely noticed, read, and remembered.

#69 Wherever you are talking, the walls probably have ears.

#70 If you have something you are tempted to "share with someone in love," go ahead and share it. They can decide if you were loving or not.

#71   Your family and organization are worth far more than any sideline love affair.

#72   Rarely is the grass greener on the other side. If you get to the other side, the original grass will probably begin to look greener.

#73   Listen to Jimmy Buffet once in a while (at least a bit every day).

#74   You are probably more okay than you think, even on a good day. You are not as bad as you think, even on your worst day.

#75   Unmailed letters to persons—even dead persons—from your past will still speak loudly. Say "thanks." Say "goodbye." Ask "why?"

#76   Look for opportunities to facilitate proper closure, whether it be to a relationship, a program, or an agreement.

#77   Consider the source.

#78 You will be the first to hear some things. Give great care to what you do with what you hear. You will be the last to hear many things. React with grace.

#79 Let handicapped persons be your friends who happen to be handicapped. You will benefit more from viewing them that way than they will.

#80 Watch the periphery of rooms, groups, and processes. Look for the marginalized and try to figure out how to include them.

#81 Try to know as women know. They usually "know" in more versatile ways than men do. Try to know as men know. Men also "know" some things that are important.

#82 The young, progressive crowd of today will be the old, stubborn crowd of tomorrow. Honor both right now.

#83 Find a mentor or two. Be a mentor to somebody someday.

#84 Bigger is not always better.

#85 Jesus was crucified by a majority vote. Sometimes numbers don't tell the whole story.

#86 Watch "Biography" on the A&E channel.

#87 Becoming too personally invested can take away your self-esteem.

#88 On building consensus, help the organization to be informed, and then get out of the way. Taking sides is dangerous.

#89 The color of the wall paint and the size of the organization's newsletter probably matter greatly to someone . . . and not at all to someone else.

#90 You won't help most people until they want help.

#91   Be a lifelong learner.

#92   False or contrived "thanks" will usually be detected.

#93   Saving the world won't work, unless you save it one person at a time.

#94   "Never teach a pig to sing. It wastes your time, and it frustrates the pig."

#95   Once in a while wander the building when it's empty. If you try, you'll learn from what it says.

#96   Even if you are a slob by nature, a clean office will save your neck occasionally. Work at it one piece of paper at a time. Periodically clean your office, straighten your book-shelves, and throw away piles that may have accumulated. A clean office is necessary when "company" is coming. Keep your mess out of sight.

#97 Find a trusted counselor and share your emotions. The exercise of it is healthy. View it as a tune-up for your psyche. Everybody needs someone to talk to—even you.

#98 People will surprise you with their interest and goodness. Remember and appreciate these glimpses of heaven. They help to smooth out the rough spots.

#99 Keep a "Feel Good" file. When folks send you a note of appreciation, or when you achieve highly, drop a remembrance in the "Feel Good" file. Read through your "Feel Good" file occasionally, but don't rely on others as the sole judges of your worth.

#100 Meet people where they are. Take people where they need to go.

#101 "The mind can only absorb what the fanny can endure."

#102 In programming, if you err, err on the side of leaving the people wanting more.

#103 When you teach, do it as learning facilitation.

#104 Assume that your people are wondering, "So what?" They are.

#105 "Most people keep their internal radio tuned to WII-FM (What's In It For Me?)."

#106 If you begin to doubt yourself, ask for help.

#107 Assume that many of your people are really saying, "Help me cope." They are.

#108 Take in a symphony concert.

#109 Visit the theater—and not just the one with 10 screens.

#110 Read some good personnel and management books.

#111 Help your organization to be relevant.

#112 Perception *is* reality. What the people think is usually their idea of truth.

#113 Be as wise as a serpent and as innocent as a dove.

#114 Days filled on your calendar are not the same as fulfilled days on your calendar.

#115 The more a person works, the more a person sweats. Nothing works like work.

#116 Success always comes in *cans*—not cannots.

#117 Fail to plan, and you plan to fail. Plan your work, and then work your plan.

#118 If you don't know where you want to go, then any route will take you there. But if you don't know where you want to go, then how will you know where you are when you get there?

#119 When you're falling on your face, you're actually moving forward.

#120 Listen to Lyle Lovett for an hour.

#121 It ain't "a big thang" unless you make it "a big thang."

#122 Big ships turn slowly. Anyone can paddle a canoe.

#123 Listen to the *Chariots of Fire* soundtrack by Vangelis.

#124 Rent three of your favorite comedy videos and take a mental health day.

#125 Don't wait until you are totally happy to laugh.

#126 Spend some time reading children's books.

#127 Anybody can be stupid, but not everybody can love stupid.

#128 Everything takes longer than you think. Every *think* should take a while, too.

#129 When in doubt, trust your gut.

#130 Define yourself. Reinvent yourself. Redefine yourself.

#131 If it ain't broke, break it. If it ain't broke, don't mess with it. If it ain't broke, delegate it. The trick is deciding.

#132 Deciding not to decide is still a decision.

#133 Read the dictionary or a thesarus for an hour each week.

#134 Listen to the Eagles for an hour.

#135 Fly a kite; climb on the monkey bars; swing in a swing.

#136 Call a friend you haven't talked to in six months or more.

#137 In everything be intentional.

#138 Be a less anxious leader.

#139 Know thyself . . . and to thine own self be true.

#140 You can get forgiveness easier than you can get permission—unless you make a habit of it. If so, soon you will get neither.

#141 You can always duplicate an event but never an experience.

#142 A man can cry when he's going at something, but never, never when he's running away.

#143 Fires left untended soon burn out.

#144 Success is going from failure to failure without loss of enthusiasm.

#145 Forgiveness is the ultimate revenge, indifference the ultimate insult.

#146 Frogs are lucky. They can eat what bugs 'em.

#147 The problem is that nobody wants to take responsibility for anything anymore. . . . But don't quote me on that.

#148 The problem isn't the main problem. The main problem is my attitude about the problem.

#149 Frustration is not having anyone to blame but yourself.

#150 Systems exist to keep things the same.

#151 Tell me; I will forget. Show me; I will remember. Involve me; I will understand.

#152 People need the most love and understanding when they least deserve it.

#153 Learn to relax!
Rest
Escape
Laugh
Alter routines
Xercise

#154 Without discipline, vision is a fantasy. Without vision, discipline is a drudgery.

#155 Change is inevitable; growth is optional.

#156 Embrace change.

#157 Build equity.

#158 Everybody is a star.

#159 When deciding whether to enlarge the facilities or organization, inform the group, but be careful how much *you* decide for the people.

#160 Let those who dare to teach never cease to learn.

#161 Zen proverb: Before enlightenment, chop wood and carry water. After enlightenment, chop wood and carry water.

#162 Today is the tomorrow that worried you yesterday. . . . And all is well.

#163 20% of the people do 80% of the work. 80% nonparticipation is *not* acceptable.

#164 Understand that it is not all about you and what you want.

#165 Learn to say, "Please," "Thank you," "I appreciate you," and "Could you help me?"

#166 Burn no bridges; build them instead.

#167 Chase some rainbows.

#168 Develop a personal mission statement that is no more than ten words in length and defines what you do.

#169 Develop a logo that is a visual representation of your mission.

#170 Let every plan and value flow from your personal mission statement. Focus on *your* personal, individual giftedness.

#171 Do what you say you will do. If you offer, mean it.

#172 Take notes during a presentation on the material *in* the presentation.

#173 Walk the building each week from a different direction. Look for what you've been missing.

#174 Never say never. *Never!*

#175 Read an entire "Far Side" calendar in one sitting.

#176 Take a moment to bite into a piece of cold, crisp, sweet watermelon . . . or thick, rich chocolate cake.

#177 Keep a pen and notecards close. You'll write more relational notes to people who "pop" into your mind if these are handy.

#178 Let your office reflect who you are. Be comfortable. Photos, mementos, and other personal items can help you take five-minute "mental" vacations. Mental vacations can refresh you and add perspective to tough decisions.

#179 Leading people to where you have never been before is very difficult.

#180 Be real. Be yourself. Be true to your call.

#181 When you are debating an issue, you and your "opponent" are weakest at the point of your assumptions.

#182 *Never* assume.

#183 The organization is becoming what the leaders are.

#184 The organization is only as strong as its weakest member.

#185 You can't short-cut the paying of dues. If you try to, it will catch up with you eventually. Choose how you will pay your dues.

#186 Keep and use self-inking stamps that read: "Confidential," "Date Received/Sent," and "File Copy."

#187 Much time and money have been spent on high-tech time management tools. The best ones to buy are the ones you'll actually use.

#188 Integrity is the hallmark by which your leadership is judged. It cannot be manipulated or falsified.

#189 Don't be falsely modest. Be grace-filled in thanking people for their kindnesses. They need to give them as much as they need for you to hear them.

#190 Don't feel too pressured to give folks an all-encompassing view of what you consider to be important. They'll see for themselves soon enough.

#191 Know your limitations *and* your strengths. Your greatest strength can be a liability.

#192 Know your ego. It will lead you in directions God never would.

#193 Invest in the community where you work. Folks can tell if your roots are shallow or deep.

#194 Lend your books and resources freely. It helps you build relationships and networks you in helpful ways with the borrowers.

#195 Learn your own needs and techniques for drawing boundaries. Poor limits quickly help to exceed your capacity for effective leadership.

#196 Be realistic about yourself and your context when drawing boundaries.

#197 We are all "fellow pilgrims" struggling together. Others will look to you for leadership, but it does not always mean you are ahead of them in all aspects of the journey.

#198 Learn names and faces as quickly as you can. To the extent that you really know your people, you will be able to join them in just about any event.

#199 You will be able to trust others only to the extent that you trust yourself.

#200 Don't play hero.

#201 Ever feel like Barney Fife? On the days you do, enjoy it.

#202 Handle any piece of paper as few times as possible. Paper is the greatest enemy of a clean office. You have four options: do, delegate, file, or toss.

#203 The telephone can be your greatest asset and your worst enemy. Learn to harness and limit this machine. (The same goes for your computer and the Internet.) Return calls 15 minutes before your lunch hour and 15 minutes before leaving for the day.

#204 Never rely, in an ultimate way, on things that plug into the wall. Always have a plan "B" in mind.

#205 Read the comics now and then. They are windows to some souls and mirrors to others.

#206 Laugh at yourself; give others permission to do so, too.

#207 In the name of nervousness, don't say funny things that may turn around on you.

#208 Find ways to let the community know that your organization is an interested and relevant citizen.

#209 Folks can tell when an organization is trying to manipulate or take over a community. Be a genuine presence.

#210 You can usually trust persons who walk around whistling. Look for them. Try it yourself.

#211 The best leader is not always the first nor the loudest voice. Learn to find the voices of leadership around you. Try not to be the first or the loudest voice.

#212 Growth always takes place on the edge of chaos.

#213 Trust the process. The journey is always valuable.

#214 Give people permission.

#215 Educators have to change as models change.

#216 A paradigm is more than 20 cents. Learn to recognize one and work with it.

#217 Evaluation is always more than numbers.

#218 Develop your own personal place of sanctuary.

#219 No one is seeking another obligation. Involve others willingly.

#220 Relationships are the keys to success.

#221 Help learners to touch, feel, taste, react, and *learn.*

#222 Read an hour of Will Rogers.

#223 Become user-friendly.

#224 If truth is truth, can you find it in a variety of ways and a variety of places?

#225 Read a biography of one of your heroes.

#226 Keep an active list of developing and potential leaders in the organization.

#227 Focus on who you are and who you are becoming. Remember who you have been.

#228 Take time to think more, feel more, understand more, and do more.

#229 Are you an artist or a mechanic? Learn to become both.

#230 Which is more important for you: program or process? Learn to become comfortable with both.

#231 Good intentions don't necessarily lead to good communication.

#232 It is okay to be bored every now and then.

#233 Don't be in the business of cloning workers.

#234 Learn to juggle—literally and figuratively. Learn to be a clown. Learn to laugh.

#235 Learn to cook . . . to write . . . to do electrical work or plumbing.

#236 Build bridges. A bridge is a structure that allows access over an obstacle.

#237 Be empathetic more than sympathetic.

#238 Discover a place where you can go to laugh. Discover a place where you can go to cry.

#239 Take a day off . . . go fishing . . . work in the yard . . . ride a carousel . . . fly a kite.

#240 Take your spouse out on a date.

#241 Make your weekends fun. Do your chores during the week.

#242 Work smarter; seek quality. Work harder; seek quality.

#243 Take an hour every Sunday night to arrange your family calendar for the coming week.

#244 Members in your organization really don't care *how* you did it in another organization.

#245 Keep your supervisor informed at all times.

#246 Never light a match to see if there is gas in your gas tank.

#247 Never pet a Doberman to see how friendly the dog is.

#248 Winners never quit. Quitters never win.

#249 Take what you've got and use it to achieve results.

#250 Good leaders need good followers. Model good leadership. Model good "followership."

#251 God created you to be a high quality performer.

#252 Find ways to turn the ordinary into the extraordinary.

#253 If you're going to walk on thin ice, you might as well dance. You never know who your true friends are until you are dancing on thin ice.

#254 Constantly ask yourself, "Am I part of the problem, part of the solution, or merely a critical spectator?"

#255 Send flowers or balloons to your spouse every now and then.

#256 Look happy.

#257 Keep quiet unless you can improve the silence.

#258 Play fair—even if others cheat. What goes around comes around.

#259 Develop a high frustration tolerance. Don't blow up or sulk. Control your feelings.

#260 Be a good sport. Lose graciously. Win even more graciously.

#261 Set realistic goals.

#262 There is always more than the tip of an iceberg. There is always more than one side of a story.

#263 Arguing with most people is like wrestling with a pig. You both get dirty—but the pig enjoys it.

#264 Become who you have been created to be.

#265 Be a person of vision. Discover what one or two overarching purposes guide your life. Your leadership may be only one of many valid expressions of that vision.

#266 What skills do you need to brush up on soon? Find a growing edge and invest in it through a learning experience.

#267 Your academic degree or diploma has an amazingly short "shelf life." If you haven't engaged in training or an educational exercise lately, find a way to become updated.

#268 You find time to do what you want to do.

#269 The best way to come across as one who "thinks on their feet" is to do your homework and then communicate your convictions when asked. Stay in touch with the lay of the land.

#270 Pass the "blessing" to someone today. While you can't substitute for missed opportunities of the past, your blessing will go a long way toward helping those you come in contact with.

#271 Say a prayer of thanks for those who helped you become the person you are.

#272 Recall the sights, sounds, smells, faces, and voices that were your roots.

#273 Rarely will you err by overcommunicating with your people. Let them know well in advance when you want them to be present for an event. Study and use good resources that update your promotion skills.

#274 Foster two-way communication between you and persons in the organization.

#275 Often you will be held accountable for those things you know, along with those things you may not know. Surround yourself with trust-worthy persons who can serve as your extra eyes and ears.

#276 Needing a supportive pick-me-up? Try to think of someone else who must need one, and get in touch with that person.

#277 Expect the best of people, and they will rise to your expectations.

#278 Be five minutes early for everything.

#279 Learn to swim upstream.

#280 Think 3-6 months ahead; plan 1-2 months ahead; be prepared 1-2 days ahead.

#281 Learn how to promote yourself without bragging or showboating. If you do something spectacular and surprise even yourself, try to act like you have done it before. If you do something spectacular and fail, keep trying. In either case, never let them see you sweat.

#282 Learn to say "no," "not right now," "yes," and "maybe."

#283 Empower others to help you do your work. Empower others to help them do their work.

#284 Give away more than you take.

#285 When you wear a nametag, wear it on your right side. This will allow people's natural eye movement to gravitate to your nametag without having to look for your name.

#286 Everyone is replaceable—especially you.

#287 If something sounds too good to be true, it probably is. Choose carefully. Some of life's greatest lessons have ended up costing dearly.

#288 There is no such thing as "the opportunity of a lifetime."

#289 There is no such thing as "get rich quick."

#290 Invest in yourself and other people. Invest in blue chip stocks and mutual funds with a good ten-year track record. Invest systematically.

#291 Set realistic goals. Have great dreams.

#292 Find ways to duplicate yourself.

#293 All that glitters is not gold.

#294 Garbage in, garbage out is true for more than computer work.

#295 Take some time to send cards to your children or other loved ones.

#296 Laugh out loud about something every day.

#297 Eat more ice cream. Sometimes eat an exotic flavor; sometimes just enjoy plain vanilla.

#298 Be spontaneous even if you have to plan for spontaneity.

#299 The best things in life are free, even though sometimes you may have to pay for them.

#300 Listen to the music of Pachelbel for an hour.

#301 Take a day and go fishing—whether you buy bait or not.

#302 Spend an hour browsing in a card shop.

#303 Spend a day playing with your own kids or babysitting for someone else's kids.

#304 When you speak, remember it is hard to be bad if you are brief. As P. T. Barnham said, "Always keep them wanting more."

#305 Most of what you worry about never happens.

#306 Spend a day on the golf course—whether you carry clubs or not. If you don't play, just walk.

#307 Always carry a notepad and a pen for writing down your ideas, dreams, goals, and thoughts. Ideas can come at the craziest times. You'll accomplish more just by writing them down. Keep a pen and pad beside your bed, too.

#308 Always have a pen and paper with you at meetings. If you don't know why, then try carrying them regularly—and you'll find out.

#309 Don't try to do everything every day. Ask yourself what two things are most important to do today, and then do those well.

#310 Pay careful attention to diet. Rationalize though you may, you really are what you eat. What you put into your body in your 20s and 30s stays with you in your 40s and 50s.

#311 Exercise at least three times a week. Put the times on your calendar and honor the commitment. Exercise is a huge stress buster.

#312 Never accept a "no" answer from someone who is not authorized to give you a "yes" response.

#313 If the tie or scarf doesn't really match the suit, don't wear it.

#314 If an invitation says RSVP, make sure you do.

#315 When you are a hammer, the only way you think you can fix problems is by pounding the nail.

#316 It's not important that you are busy every day. It's important that you are busy with the right things every day.

#317 You will be recognized more for your ability to work with people than to work with paper.

#318 Some folks look forward to the future with an "if only" attitude. Some folks look to the past with a "woulda, shoulda, coulda" attitude. Wise people live in the here and now and do their best every day.

#319 You make a living by what you get. You make a life by what you live.

#320 Luck happens when preparation and opportunity meet.

#321 When you start to think about changing others, remember how difficult it is for you to change.

#322 Here is the essence of teamwork: If anything fails, I did it. If anything happens pretty good, we did it. If anything is a complete success, then you did it.

#323 Some folks see two kinds of people in the world: those who do the work and those who take credit. Be a part of the first group.

#324 Motivation is always a one-on-one event. Motivate one person and one more person and one more person, and soon you have motivated the group.

#325 You are called to manage the process, not the content. You can share and lead your group about what and how to lead, but you can never control what they say or do. If you try, you will drive yourself crazy and lose good workers.

#326 When people push you with constructive criticism, it means they have confidence in you.

#327 Nobody likes a know-it-all; nobody trusts a do-it-all.

#328 There are five types of people in any organization: risktakers, caretakers, undertakers, joytakers, and joymakers. Whatever else you are, always be a "joymaker."

#329 Much of the work you do may be outdated, outmoded, or irrelevant. The trick is to find the things that really matter to the organization. Do the right things well, and you will thrive.

#330 Never give bad news to anyone on Friday.

#331 Recognizing people in the organization should be a part of your daily routine.

#332 Never end a motivational speech with "thank you" or "in conclusion."

#333 Work on your voice quality before delivering your next speech.

#334 Ignore the excuse and attack the problem. Don't get caught up in arguing or debating the validity of excuses. Focus on the person and the solution.

#335 Start a reading club among several colleagues. Find out what they are reading and share with them what you are reading.

#336 Communication is 90% of everything you do. Practicing good communication is like trying to stick Jell-O to the wall.

#337 If a decision has already been made, don't call a meeting to ask permission.

#338 When you criticize someone, do it orally. When you praise someone, do it orally and in writing. When you criticize someone, do it privately. When you praise someone, do it publically.

#339 People don't want pat solutions; they want creative responses to their questions and personalized suggestions to their problems.

#340 Committees were made for the decision-making process because that way no one has to take the blame.

#341 Excellence is doing your job well even when you don't feel like it or even when you don't have to.

#342 Solutions to problems are not always found in new brilliant and creative approaches. Sometimes they are discovered in tweaking old and proven ideas.

#343 Failure is never fatal; success is never final.

#344 The modern leader's role is not that of being boss and giving orders. Rather, leadership is leading people to make decisions through self-motivation, creativity, and interest in their work.

#345 Today's exceptional leaders soak up information realizing that they can learn from anyone. They are constantly looking for ways to make things better.

#346 As you work with the two main groups in the organization, you will find that young adults want to change the world and older adults want to change the young adults.

#347 When people share their concerns with you, they trust you enough to wait for your understanding of their situation and suggestions on dealing with it.

#348 Wisdom comes from learning while living.

#349 The people who scare me the most aren't the ones who say, "I'm angry." Those who scare me the most are those who say, "I don't get mad; I get even."

#350 What gets measured becomes important.

#351 Hold yourself accountable for outcomes. Model leadership by setting your own deadlines and sticking to them and by setting quality goals and achieving them.

#352 Focus on a higher power.

#353 When purchasing equipment, spend extra dollars for a good copier and an even better printer for your computer. Always spend money that makes you look good in print.

#354 If you want to be a change agent, first make sure you know what you want to change. Second, make sure you know where you are going with the change.

#355 Create a personal advisory board. Enlist several people with whom you work closely. Once a quarter ask them for personal feedback. Ask: "What am I doing well?" "What do I need to do better?" Take their feedback constructively and positively. Reflect on what they say, learn from what they tell you, and change what you can.

#356 On the days when work is not fair, remember that's why they call it work. If you enjoyed every day you come to work, it wouldn't be work; it would be play, and you don't get paid for playing. It's how you work when things aren't fair that justify the dollars you make.

#357 Keep an ongoing wish list . . . things you wish you had, books you'd like to read, people you'd like to meet. As you dream creatively, you'll find many of your wishes coming true. If you don't write your wishes down, they'll eventually be forgotten. Put a star by those wishes that come true.

#358 "Leadership is thousands of nudges."

#359 Spend some time surfing the Internet, but don't spend all your time out there. You can easily waste a day just having fun in virtual reality.

#360 If you don't have time to do it right the first time, you sure don't have time to do it over. Do it perfect next time. Do your best this time.

#361 If you surround yourself with great people, then you will accomplish great things.

#362 Pay attention to your appearance. There's nothing more distracting than a $5 haircut— unless maybe it's a pair of unshined shoes.

#363 Spend ten minutes every day reading a joke book or the comics.

#364 Be unconventional. Find one or two ways to go against the grain. You will sharpen your creative skills and be recognized as a creative and innovative person.

#365 Go in the direction you think you ought to be going. As you follow that direction, the way will continually be made clearer to you.

#366 Do your work because you love it. If you are excited about it, you will do it better and better and better. Always do the work you dread first, and then spend the rest of your time each day enjoying what you do.

#367 In every success there must be a high tolerance for failure. If you learn from failure, it is not failure at all but education. You only fail when you quit.

#368 You can never go back and rewrite your past. Learn from what you can and forget the rest. Accept grace and grow forward.

#369 You are never alone. Use all the brain power around you and in your own head.

#370 Don't dump on other people. Never ask someone to do what you are not willing to do yourself.

#371 Work daily at keeping a positive attitude. If you can smile through problems, mistakes, and stress, you will eventually succeed. Believe that you are going to win, and eventually you will.

#372 Work hard at working with others, being consistent, setting attainable goals, visualizing success, and doing things now.

#373 Build trust.

#374 Build relationships based on trust. Be patient and intentional.

#375 Build a team by maximizing the strengths of members.

#376 Address concerns with individuals directly rather than in the group.

#377 Notice even small improvements and affirm them.

#378 Add a new word to your vocabulary daily.

#379 Learn to lead, follow, and team; and know when each is needed.

#380 Welcome others' opinions.

#381 Encourage questions.

#382 Understand that "junk costs" can apply to any kind of resources. Know when to persevere, when to wait, and when to drop an issue.

#383 Find out who influences your organization. Let them help you communicate your dreams and vision.

#384 Work early on projects. Every hour you spend planning will save you two later on.

#385 Remember that ongoing evaluation is an essential part of the planning process.

#386 Follow your plan. Planning is valuable only when it is used and revised; it is useless lying on a shelf.

#387 Look for a way for everyone to win in any situation.

#388 Establish core values with your team. Set the example by honoring them.

#389 Never say anything negative about one team member to another—or to anyone else.

#390 Treat others the way you want to be treated.

#391 Offer more grace than judgment.

#392 When employees fail, recognize that part of the responsibility is the supervisor's—for training, communication, and placement.

#393 Meet individual team members' needs as much as possible in the context of what is best for the whole team.

#394 Plan time for team recreation, and sometimes include family members.

#395 Celebrate . . . completed projects, anniversaries, birthdays, family milestones.

#396 Welcome new ideas.

#397 Become comfortable saying, "I don't know, but I'll find out."

#398 Spend time equipping others.

#399 Help co-workers achieve their fullest potential. Always give them the benefit of a doubt.

#400 Dare to be innovative.

#401 Look for good in everyone.

#402 Delegate both tasks and responsibilities.

#403 Provide all the resources to help team members succeed.

#404 Budget time and money for training.

#405 Build your team by sharing dreams, work, and joys.

#406 Look for possibilities.

#407 Use technology to enhance what you do— not to impress others.

#408 Read in your areas of interest, new areas, and fiction.

#409 Be flexible in your work and in your life.

#410 Accept people; seek to modify behavior as needed.

#411 Understand existing circumstances before making changes.

#412 Listen to criticism.

#413 Develop a plan for learning new skills, viewpoints, ideas, and areas of interest.

#414 Discover your own tendency to focus on tasks or people. Find ways to achieve balance.

#415 Expand your influence through writing, mentoring, teaching, and equipping.

#416 Start and end meetings on time.

#417 Have a written agenda for every meeting.

#418 Have meetings only when they are needed.

#419 Make eye contact when you talk to people.

#420 Develop good listening skills. Listen actively.

#421 Use people's names when you talk with them.

#422 Use humor only when it is at no one's expense—except occasionally your own.

#423 Be careful with teasing or sarcasm. The trait you joke about may be a sensitive area.

#424 Be willing to laugh at yourself.

#425 Be a good steward of your resources as well as others' time and money.

#426 Find positive ways to communicate the work you do to those who may not know.

#427 Investigate how your role is perceived and take steps to redirect any misconceptions.

#428 Recognize the types of power you have— personal, position, knowledge—and use your power responsibly.

#429 Discover what motivates and rewards people. Build into their jobs ways to meet their needs.

#430 Use professional tests to help team members understand their own and one another's leadership styles, personality types, and ways of thinking.

#431 The most difficult position to fill is the one with an ineffective person already in it.

#432 Become childlike. Develop innocence, energy, and expectancy.

#433 Give yourself permission to play. Play raises your energy level, frees you from cynicism and pessimism, and moves you from "stuck" places.

#434 Never pigeon-hole others. Give people permission to grow.

#435 When you start a new job, they give you a gun and all the rat shot you want. They also give you five elephant bullets. The trick is in discerning rats from elephants. You only get five elephant shots. If you shoot rats with elephant bullets, you come across as being out of control. If you shoot elephants with rat shot, you only make the elephants mad.

#436 Look for "historians" among your workers. Folks who have seen some laps around your organization's calendar can be invaluable when trying to recapture some of the subtleties of your work. Take time to hear how they remember events and policies unfolding over time. They may confirm your records and memories, or they may have a totally new take on things.

#437 Be prepared for meetings by anticipating the tough questions and the easy ones. If you've already asked yourself those questions, you're a leg up on answering them when it counts.

#438 Accept resignations with grace. You'll be tempted to skip ahead in the conversation to scenarios that deal with replacement. But take the time to work through the departure first. Learn from the person who's leaving what went well and what didn't.

#439 If an employee is leaving for a job that represents a positive move, then honor that person in front of her co-workers. Send positive signals about your care for employees' advancement.

#440 Learn to use both sides of your brain. Consistently using only one side of your brain is like jumping on one foot for the rest of your life.

#441 The only "bad" style of communicating is the one you use all the time.

#442 "Lead, follow, or get out of the way."

#443 Explore the least used strategies, and then get out of the way and let empowered persons do the job.

#444 A blind hog finds an ear of corn now and then. Never count on being the blind hog, but be honest and thankful when you are.

#445 Let your word be your bond. Let forms and contracts merely serve as explanations of that bond.

#446 Always conduct exit interviews with employees who are leaving. You will uncover good information that will make you a better supervisor and make your organization stronger. Allow departing employees the freedom to speak candidly about the "good, bad, and ugly" of their experiences in your organization.

#447 Networking is a way of life in today's sectors. Make contacts in as many areas as possible. You never know when a wonderful opportunity will come your way because of an acquaintance you've made. Remember to help others along the way, too.

#448 Synergy works. Brainstorming ideas and feeding off the energy of the group is a wonderful approach to creativity. Letting the group find a million solutions to a problem is a wonderful approach to problem solving. The success of any project is to involve as many people as possible. You will benefit from their ideas, energy, and enthusiasm.

#449 Ask yourself about your own personal definition of "success." Is it strictly numbers based? Is it materially based? Is it values or performance based? Imbalance toward any one area leaves you vulnerable to failures in the other areas.

#450 Learn current technology. Becoming computer literate, fax machine able, and voice mail savvy will help you become much more productive. You will be amazed at how much more you can accomplish when you are comfortable with technological advances.

#451 The word "but" really means "no." Try to avoid using this word when brainstorming or discussing differing views. While you may say on the one hand something positive, as soon as you say "but," you have essentially said, "no." Find ways to be positive even when you must say "no."

#452 Pay attention to your telephone manners.

#453 An effective worker does the right things. An efficient worker does things right. An effective leader knows how to get a worker to do both.

#454 When you get angry, do not lose your temper. There is nothing worse than letting your anger control you.

#455 "Learn to walk, and you can learn to dance. Learn to talk, and you can learn to sing."

#456 Being good is never good enough. Being the best is rarely achieved. Win little victories and celebrate.

#457 There is no competition among lighthouses. Candles never lose their light by giving their flames away.

#458 Be so good in what you do that you get the attention of everyone else. If you can't be good, hang around people who are.

#459 Working together works better than working alone. And, working alone works better than not working at all.

#460 Read *People* magazine at least once a month.

#461 Watch "Oprah" at least once a week.

#462 Let your passion for doing a job flow through you just like a concert pianist lets music flow through him.

#463 The closer the deadline, the harder the work—and the easier to make mistakes.

#464 Read a book of Yogi Berra sayings. There's wisdom in his words . . . or maybe not.

#465 Take power naps. When you feel sleepy or drowsy, take a ten-minute break and nap.

#466 Challenge employees never to bring complaints without having two solutions for each complaint.

#467 The older I become, the younger those older than I become.

#468 Do the right things right.

#469 Brainstorm with members of the organization when stuck trying to find a solution. Write down all responses, even the silly ones. These will be clues to a wonderful solution if you look with intentionality.

#470 Allow your workers to be flexible. Workers who have some flexibility in work are happier and more productive.

#471 When greeting people, focus on the color of their eyes. This will help you pay attention to those you are greeting and keep you from looking over their shoulder to greet others around you.

#472 If you say you have an "open-door" policy, make sure your door is open. If you say you manage "by walking around," you best be seen in the halls.

#473 Change the masthead and layout of your publications at least once every 18 months. Publications become stale when you leave them the same way for too long.

#474 If at first you do succeed, try not to be surprised. When you do succeed, try to act like you've done it before.

#475 Follow the work of Jimmy Carter. Read his books.

#476 Invest heavily in building the loyalty of others. If persons in your organization know you will take care of them, they will take care of you. If you teach teamwork, you had better be a team player.

#477 Where there is bad news to be given, involve the minimal number of persons necessary in a meeting. There is no need to "ambush" the party. In situations where you have doubt about the integrity or comprehension of the party, find a way to involve a colleague so there is an extra set of ears in the meeting.

#478 Try to include all pertinent parties in meetings. This saves communication effort and time in the long run. It also gets the proper people on-board when you need them in the mix and builds solidarity in the process.

#479 Communication isn't over until the feedback has been received.

#480 Folks just seem to have differences in how they perceive what you may think was communicated clearly. Memos and notes serve as good backups in communication. Better to have too many records than to come up short.

#481 Don't give persons responsibility they have not been empowered to carry out. Help supervisees by making sure they are up to speed on their job and that the necessary structures of support are in place as they have need.

#482 Being new in an organization is like being the prize hog at the state fair. You can presume that folks are walking around you trying to see what all the fuss is over. Don't shoot yourself in the foot by trying to be something other than you are. Be considerate of the need to build relationships in the context of your newness.

#483 Take time when you delegate. Set up new responsibilities intentionally. Communicate clearly with all who will be impacted by the new arrangement.

#484 Leadership is most often an earned position. Very little of your inherited power will serve you for the long haul. Enduring leadership is earned by consistency and hard work. Fighting this principle will only make things harder.

#485 Be present for your people and your organization. If your schedule makes you geographically absent, then stay connected adequately. Use technology and relationships to stay plugged in with your people.

#486 When you succeed at work or in life, don't quit your "day job." Athletes who suddenly get huge endorsement deals often trail off in their careers because they neglect what got them the endorsements in the first place— their on-field results. Managers sometimes do this, too.

#487 Find a way to leave a legacy. Charter a Habitat for Humanity chapter, teach something, or start a community initiative. You will ask yourself at some point what your life has been all about. Stock portfolios, inflated bank accounts, and large companies rarely seem to be adequate answers.

#488 Try to develop a sense of "timing" about life. It's all a matter of perspective when wise judgments are needed. Sometimes it's good to jump. Other times you need to wait.

#489 The one who empties your garbage can each day will probably know whether you worked hard or not.

#490 Beat the curve by seeing how you can "do it differently" the first time.

#491 Travel through this life lightly. Things that are not of ultimate importance tend to weigh you down.

#492 Let your "yes" be yes and your "no" be no.

#493 You'll never get all you deserve—and you'll never deserve all you get.

#494 You can *never* be best friends with the boss.

#495 If you get a day off, take it. If not, learn to enjoy your weekends.

#496 Run personal errands on your own time.

#497 Try to maintain a clear sense of understanding for what your team or organization is working to accomplish. Tell that story around the building. If the guy pushing the cleaning cart understands why your building is used, his job takes on much more meaning. If his job has more meaning, he will probably do it better. Chances are, if he understands your mission, the middle and upper-level folks do, too.

#498 Try to be the stabilizing presence in a world trying to cope.

#499 If people think you're lazy, you are. If they think you are a hard worker, you are. If you think they hate you, they do. If you think they love you, they do.

#500 Just when you thought you were finished, you get more ideas and have to start all over again.

#501 Leaders are not born; they are made. Be one; make one. Emerge!

––––––

Now it's your turn.

In the next few months keep track of your own leadership motivators. Write them down on the following pages and refer to them consistently.

Grow for it! Emerge!